SUCCESSFUL SPORTS

ATHLETICS

Tony Ward

Heinemann

First published in Great Britain by
Heinemann Publishers (Oxford) Ltd,
Halley Court, Jordan Hill, Oxford OX2 8EJ

MADRID ATHENS PARIS
FLORENCE PRAGUE WARSAW
PORTSMOUTH NH CHICAGO SAO PAULO
SINGAPORE TOKYO MELBOURNE AUCKLAND
IBADAN GABORONE JOHANNESBURG

This edition published 1996

Designed by Ron Kamen, Green Door Design Ltd, Basingstoke, England
Illustrated by Barry Atkinson

Printed in China

00 99 98 97 96
10 9 8 7 6 5 4 3 2 1

ISBN 0 431 07441 0

British Library Cataloguing in Publication Data

Ward, Tony
Athletics - (Successful Sports Series)
I. Title II. Series
796.42

Acknowledgements
The Publishers would like to thank the following for permission to reproduce photographs:
Allsport: pp. 5, 13, 15, 16, 19, 20, 22, 23, 25, 26, 27, 28, 29; Colorsport: title page and p. 24; Sporting Pictures: pp. 9, 12; Meg Sullivan: pp. 4, 8, 10, 11, 14, 17, 18, 21.

All other photographs supplied by the Author.

Cover photograph © Allsport/Gray Mortimore

The cover photo shows Linford Christie racing in 1992.
The title page photo shows Roger Black anchoring the Great Britain 4 x 400 metres relay team to success in the 1994 World Cup at Crystal Palace.

The Publishers and Author would like to thank the Run, Jump, Throw Club, run by Maureen Jones and based in Crawley, for help with the photographs.

Contents

The birth of athletics

People have probably run races against each other as a sport for thousands of years. As long ago as about 700BC, the Greek writer of the *Iliad* told the story of a famous foot race. The first organized athletics **meetings** took place in ancient Greece as part of the **Olympic Games**. The Games included running and jumping competitions, and throwing the discus and the javelin. Later there was also a five-event competition called the **pentathlon**.

These early Games were stopped in AD393 because of cheating and other dishonest behaviour. In mid-nineteenth century Europe, athletics as a sport started again in the schools and universities. After a visit to see interested sportsmen in Britain, the Frenchman Baron Pierre de Coubertin decided to restart the Olympic Games. The first modern Olympics, including many of the well-known **track** and **field** athletic events, took place in Athens, Greece in 1896. Apart from the world war years, the Olympic Games have been held every four years since then. The track and field athletics events have always been major Olympic sports, with women's athletics entering the Olympics in 1928.

Young athletes warming up. It is important to do stretching exercises as well as jogging before competition and training.

The glittering opening ceremony at the 1992 Olympic Games in Barcelona, Spain.

Equipment

Getting started in athletics is not expensive. The most important equipment a beginner needs in any of the events is a good pair of training shoes. Trainers should fit comfortably and protect the feet from injury. Good shoe and sport shops can give advice. If you decide to take up an athletic event seriously, then you may need spiked shoes. The only clothing required are t-shirts and shorts, and a track suit for keeping warm. For those taking up field events such as javelin, discus and shot put, schools and local clubs usually provide beginners with suitable equipment.

Many young people get interested in athletics while they are at school. To improve your skills and have a chance to enter competitions, you may want to join a local club. Clubs can supply specialist advice as well as chances for extra training. Before joining a club, find out as much as possible about it. Make sure that there is proper training by experienced coaches, regular entries by club members into competitions, good **facilities** and a happy atmosphere. Having fun and not specializing too early are key to enjoying athletics. International athletes often say 'I'll retire when the enjoyment goes'.

To see if you would like to start training in an athletic event, you can take part in the 'taster' sessions run by the British Athletic Federation during its Startrack weeks. Usually held just after a major championship, these weeks give you a chance to go along to a local **stadium** and try a whole variety of events.

Safety first

Warming-up and cooling-down are very important to keep you injury free. Exercise or jogging before training or competing can do the trick. Jogging slowly for a few minutes afterwards is equally vital.

Stadiums, surfaces and safety

Athletics offers the greatest variety of any sport. The two main divisions are the field events and the track events. Field events usually take place on the field in the centre of the stadium and include javelin, shot put, discus, hammer, triple jump, pole vaulting, high jump and long jump. The track events are all those that include running, and these usually take place on a track which circles the central field. The two exceptions are the marathon and walking events. Most of the time they take place outside of the stadium.

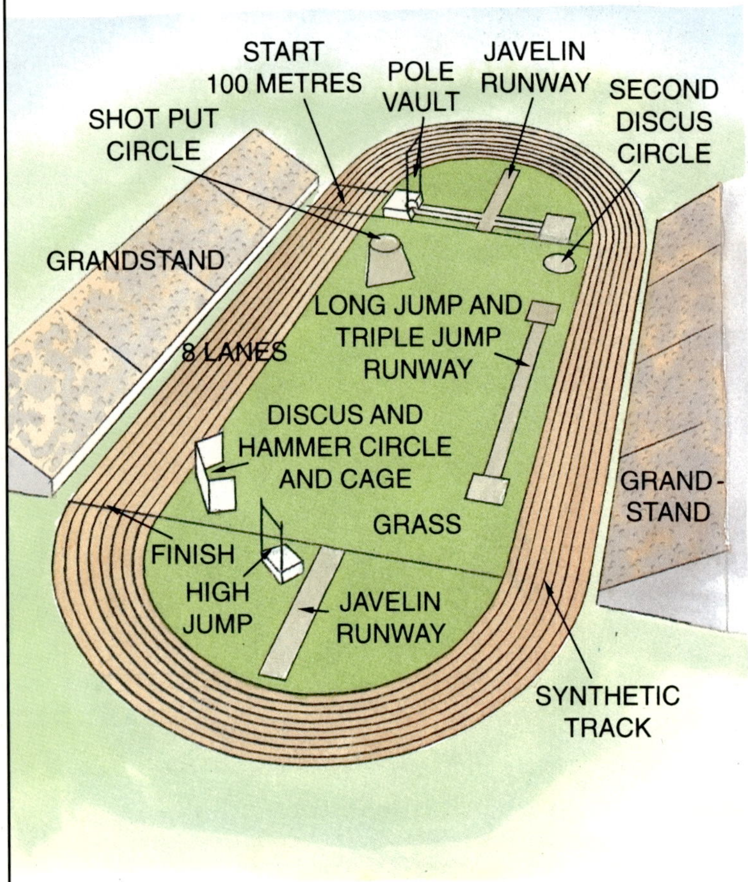

Layout of a typical stadium.

An important stadium used for international events can hold up to 100,000 spectators. The running tracks and runways are usually made of a **synthetic** rubberized material and the throwing surface take-off areas are concrete. Tracks used to be made of **cinder**. The first Olympics held on a synthetic surface was at Mexico City in 1968, and nowadays this type of surface has become the most widespread. A major stadium, like the Crystal Palace Stadium in London, has an eight-lane, 400-metre running track. It also has a long **straight** for the **sprints** and hurdles races. Because of the problems wind can cause, a big stadium like Crystal Palace will have runways and landing areas at both ends, as well as javelin runways and throwing circles at each end of the stadium. This ensures the safety of the athletes, officials and spectators.

At school and most local club meetings, starting, timekeeping and scoring are still carried out by hand. However, the most up-to-date electronic and computer-assisted methods are now used at national and international level. For example, long jump and triple jump are measured by a modern device that does not require a tape measure and the results are produced by a computer.

The famous Olympic Stadium in Munich, site of the 1972 Olympic Games.

Because the throwing **implements** used in field athletics can be very dangerous, it is important that in training and in competition safety rules are followed very strictly. For example, in training, group throwing often takes place. It is very important that all the throws are completed before the implements are collected from their landing places. Spectators need to stand well behind the throwers and should be alert at all times. No throwing should ever take place without a teacher or a coach in charge.

Safety first

At all times, especially during training sessions, athletes should pay attention to coaches and officials and be aware of what is going on around them.

Safety is also important in the jumping events. The landing beds for the high jump and the pole vault need to be of good foam, and in the long and triple jump, the sand in the pits should be well-raked and thick enough.

Running is the key

Learning to run at speed is an important skill in all athletic events. It is at the core of all other **techniques**. In events like the marathon and the 100 metres it is obvious that good running skills are vital. Speed is also a basic skill needed in all the athletic sports from triple jump to shot putting.

All jumpers and throwers need to learn the special techniques for their event. A good technique will make the most of their approach to the height they are jumping or the distance they are throwing. However, good specialist technique is not worth anything unless it is combined with speed and power. This is what good running skills can bring to the athlete. No energy should be wasted on unnecessary action, and all movement must be directed forward. Shoulders, arms and legs must work together with the eyes looking ahead and the head kept upright.

Speed on the runway is essential for all good long-jumpers.

Carl Lewis of the USA and Heike Dreschler of Germany are two great long-jumpers who are also champion runners. They excel in the short distances or sprints. Colin Jackson and Tony Jarrett are world-class hurdlers who are also members of the Great Britain sprint **relay** running team. Even while carrying a fibreglass pole, Sergey Bubka, the Ukrainian world record holder for the pole vault, could match most young sprinters running 40 metres. All these top athletes have realized the importance of speed running and have benefited from being fast.

Another skill that all sportspeople need to develop, not only those involved in athletics, is how to avoid **tension**. Tension is a great enemy which tightens the muscles and slows movement. Over the last ten or twenty metres of a sprint race you can see the runners stiffen or 'tie up' as the tension overcomes them. To fight tension you need to be fit, relaxed and confident. Keeping relaxed throughout a race right up to the end is one of the greatest skills of most successful runners. Watch Linford Christie in a television slow-motion replay of a 100 metres race. From start to finish he is perfectly relaxed. His muscles ripple and his cheeks wobble like jelly. Years of training and preparation have taught him how to relax in mind and body.

Linford Christie showing relaxation at top speed in winning the 1993 world 100m title in Stuttgart.

ATHLETICS FACTS

American Carl Lewis has excelled as an all-round athlete because of his speed. At the World Championships in the ten years from 1983 to 1993, he won gold medals in three 100 metres, two long jumps and three relay races.

Sprinting, middle-distance and distance running

Running is the most popular of all athletic events and everyone can have a go from a toddler to a pensioner. At the top levels of the sport the fastest men can travel 100 metres at 22.84 mph and the fastest women can do the same distance at 21.35 mph. The best marathon runners cover their 26.2 mile course at 12.42 mph. The speeds for the distances in between vary, but each requires different techniques and training.

A sprint finish. It is essential to think about sprinting through and well beyond the finish.

Sprinting

The sprint distances run in competition in athletics are 100, 200 and 400 metres. At each distance the athlete attempts to maintain maximum speed for the longest period of time. In all sprint races it is the athlete who is slowing down the least by the end of the race who wins.

A fast start is vital in sprinting, especially at 100 metres. Because of this, starting practice is very important. There are three commands: 'On your marks', 'Set' and then the firing of the gun for the start. If one of the runners moves off before the gun that is a known as a false start. Each runner is allowed one false start. A runner who makes two false starts in one race is **disqualified**.

In sprint racing, the start position used by the runners is called the **crouch start**. The runner kneels down on one knee with arms stretched out in front with the fingertips of both hands touching the track just behind the start line.

The front foot rests on the ground or **starting block** and the rear kneeling leg bends at a right angle with the knee on the track. On the start command 'Set' the athlete rises up so that the hips are at normal running height and on hearing the gun, powers out of the blocks. Bad concentration at this stage of a race can spoil a runner's performance.

In the 200 and 400 metres races, athletes have to learn how to sprint around a bend staying in their lanes. The athletes start in **echelon** in these races so that each will run an equal distance. For a longer sprint distance like the 400 metres, **pace judgement** is important. If the pace is set too fast at the beginning, the runner is likely to run out of energy and go too slowly at the end of the race.

'On your marks'. Hands behind the line, head in natural alignment and full concentration all show a good starting position.

Middle distance and distance

Middle-distance races of 800 and 1500 metres require a good deal of **stamina** as well as speed. The greatest runners, such as the Moroccan Noureddine Morceli or the South African Elena Meyer, can hold records and win races at a variety of distances because of their good staying power. Training and working on **tactics** are very important features of preparation for running the middle-distance races. Training ideas have changed over the years. Now most middle-distance runners practise on the track and also do cross-country and road training.

The long-distance races run at track meets are the 5000 and the 10,000 metres. For many years these distances have been the speciality of runners from the countries of East Africa. The most successful, like the famous Kip Keino, were born at high altitudes so their bodies have developed the ability to carry more oxygen in the blood. This is a great advantage in long-distance running. Also many of the African runners had to travel long distances by foot to and from school every day – the perfect training for a future running career!

Pointers

Watch a world-class sprinter like the Russian Irina Privalova and notice her high knee lift and her relaxed arm action when running.

Hurdling and steeplechasing

Hurdling is a track race run over obstacles. There are three hurdles races in an athletics programme. Usually the shorter the race, and the higher the hurdle, the more important good technique becomes. In hurdling, the distances run and the heights of the hurdles are different for men and women runners. Men run 110 metres over hurdles 106.7 cm high and women run 100 metres over 84 cm hurdles. Junior competitions and school races have shorter distances and lower hurdle heights because of the junior competitors' smaller size. A 400 metres race also has ten flights of hurdles for both men and women runners, but the men go over hurdles 91.4 cm high while the women go over 76.2 cm hurdles.

Colin Jackson in full cry. Note the high pull through of the rear leg, the lean forward, and the lead leg dipping down quickly to the track to carry on running.

Sprint hurdlers run three strides between each of the ten hurdles. The good hurdler rises to the obstacle and then gets back onto the track into the normal sprinting position as quickly as possible. This is because time spent in the air is wasted in a hurdles race. Speed can only be gathered when you are in contact with the ground. The best hurdlers move their arms and legs around the hurdle, but keep their body in virtually the same position, as when they are sprinting.

Watch a slow motion replay of a good hurdler such as Great Britain's Colin Jackson and you can see how an expert does it. The head and body do not rise up from the running position as he crosses the hurdles.

The dominant Kenyans in the lead at the steeplechase water-jump.

As his front (**leading**) leg goes up and over the hurdle, he leans forward to keep his balance and his back (**trailing**) leg curls sideways to clear the obstacle. To do this a hurdler has to be very **supple**. Special training exercises are used to help the body bend into these awkward positions.

The stride pattern when running between hurdles is very important in the 400 metres since the hurdles are further apart. It is also a great advantage to be able to lead with either leg so you have the choice of taking an even number of strides between the obstacles. One of the best-ever hurdlers at this event is the British world record holder Sally Gunnell. As part of her race tactics she regularly changes from fifteen to sixteen strides between hurdles at a fixed point in the race because she can go over a hurdle with either leg first.

The steeplechase is run over 3000 metres. It has 28 hurdles to be cleared as well as a water-jump with a hurdle just in front of it that the runners have to go over seven times. At the present time only men run this race but it is planned to add it to the women's track events by the end of the century. The world's best steeplechasers, like the world's best long-distance runners, come from Kenya.

Jumping basics

The jumping events in field athletics are the high jump, the long jump, the triple jump and the pole vault. The athletes competing in these four events try to gain the best height or the longest length by using their own power combined with special techniques. The power that goes into a jump comes from the **approach run**.

Getting as much height off the board as is possible in the long jump.

In the long and the triple jump, an athlete's approach ends on a **take-off board**. The jumper must take off from exactly the right position on or behind the board or the jump does not count. In the high jump and the pole vault, the position for take-off is not marked, but doing it at the best point is still important. If the take-off is good, the athlete will be at the highest position just as the bar is crossed. If the take-off is early or late, then the top of the curve of the jump will come before or after the bar is reached and it may be knocked off. Watch the athletes competing in the jumps. You can see them constantly practising their run-ups to make sure they have them right.

ATHLETICS FACTS

Currently, the only jumping events in which women can officially compete are the long jump, the high jump and the triple jump.

Wind conditions in the stadium can affect run-ups as well as the jumps themselves. A head wind slows the jumper down while a following wind will speed the jumper up. A following wind of faster than two metres per second for either a long jump or a triple jump will make any records gained **invalid**.

Safety first

Never practise the high jump or pole vault without a proper landing bed.

Power training to gain strength and speed is an important skill needed in good jumping. Many athletes do not do enough power training because they prefer to spend their time improving their technique. Many years ago an American jumper told his British opponent how much he liked the man's technique, but how much more he liked his own heights! This is an important lesson. No matter how good your technique, no matter how good you look technically, you still need the power to go with it.

International jumpers and vaulters use weights to gain muscle strength, especially in the legs. Younger athletes can benefit from bounding and jumping exercises. Even running up the stairs is good power training.

Steve Smith clears the bar with the Fosbury style in the high jump. Note the excellent arch of his body.

Jumping events

All the jumping events at an athletics meet take place on the field using specially prepared foam or sand landing pits. In the high jump and the pole vault, the goal is to jump as high as possible over a raised bar balanced horizontally across the top of two upright posts. In the long jump and the triple jump, the athletes try to jump as far forward as possible.

Michelle Griffiths getting good height in the triple jump.

The long jump

This event consists of a sprint run-up followed by a jump as far forward as possible, with the competitor landing in a sand-filled pit. A bad take-off can lead to disqualification while a bad landing can reduce the length measured. In most competitions, each athlete gets to make three or six jump **attempts** with the best jump counting. The long jump used to be known as the broad jump.

The triple jump

This was originally known as the hop-step and jump which perfectly describes the action of the competitor. The sprint approach is the same as the long jump but the first two jumps also take place on the runway area. The final jump starts at the end of the runway and finishes as far forward in the sand pit as possible. For the first two jumps the competitor takes off and lands on one foot, but on the final jump both feet land together in the pit. The distance is measured from the beginning of the first jump and each athlete usually gets three or six attempts.

The high jump

Athletes are allowed to run toward the high jump from the large circular run up area at any angle and can jump using any style they want. They must take off from one foot. What counts is not knocking the bar off at the height being attempted. Jumpers are allowed three attempts at a height and if they fail to clear the bar, then the highest they have already cleared counts as their best. Over the years competitors in this event have tried various ways of approach and jumping styles to get just that little bit higher. Probably the most well-known of these is the Fosbury flop. It is named after the American Dick Fosbury who first used the technique in competition in the late 1960s. Instead of using one of the straddling styles where one leg and then the other goes over, this was a head-first technique with the jumper's back arching over the bar. All top-class competitors now use a type of Fosbury flop.

Early learning of the Fosbury style in the high jump.

The pole vault

This is the only jumping event that requires any equipment: a long, thin fibreglass pole. Pole vaulters sprint down an approach runway while holding the pole to one side at shoulder height using both hands. As they get near to the pit, they stick one end of the pole down into a special metal box-shaped hole in the runway. Using the bending and springing action of the pole, vaulters launch into the air feet first, still holding on to the pole with both hands. As the pole straightens up, they give one final twist and push with their hands against the pole for added height and then let go, hopefully having cleared the bar. Pole vaulters also get three attempts at a height to successfully cross the bar.

Throwing basics

The throwing events in field athletics are the shot put, the discus, the hammer and the javelin. In all these events, the goal of the competitor is to throw the implement as far as possible without **fouling**. Speed is transferred to the implement by the competitor using the power of the throwing arm. This power is a combination of the strength of the athlete and the technique used in the lead up to the throw.

Learning the shot put. This is the ideal position at the front of the circle. Young athletes practise a 'standing put'.

Three of the four throwing events begin with the competitor standing in a start area known as the circle. It is inside the circle that the build up of power must take place if the thrower is to be successful. In the discus and the hammer the speed generated by the athlete rotating across the circle helps throw the implement a long distance. Shot putters build up speed and power in a forward glide across the circle. The transfer of the speed and power to the implement occurs when the athlete stops and the implement continues to move.

The transfer of speed and power in javelin throwing is more like that in the jumping events because they build during a run up. The throwing arm transfers the speed of the legs into the javelin when the athlete stops and throws.

Power can increase through strength training. This can be done by weight training where the athlete gradually increases the weight of the objects lifted. In Greek mythology, Myron lifted a bull above his head every day from his birth and his strength grew. Athletics coaches don't recommend bull lifting but weight training does help increase muscle bulk and strength. This type of training should not start until the mid-teens and should always be supervised.

Safety is clearly of great importance at throwing events. No one wants to be involved in an accident with a hammer or a javelin! Throwing areas are always roped off and special high-fenced 'cages' are built around the circle for the discus and hammer events at major meetings. At school and club level, in training and also at small competitions everyone needs to pay attention to the special risks.

Here are five rules that should always be followed when dealing with the throwing events:

1 Be alert at all times.
2 Never throw implements in training unless there is a teacher or a coach present.
3 Keep behind the throwing area until everyone has thrown.
4 Do not fetch implements until instructed to do so by a teacher or coach.
5 Never fool about in training or competition.

Yuri Syedykh (Russia), one of the greatest hammer throwers of all time, speeds across the circle.

Throwing events

The throwing events give an opportunity for those that are a bigger build to take part in an exciting and satisfying activity. Currently male athletes participate in all four throwing events, but women do not throw the hammer internationally. In all the throws, the implement must land inside a **designated** area in order for the throw to be measured. Each competitor will get three or six throws with the best one counting.

The shot put

A shot is a metal ball which the competitor, using one hand, pushes away from a start position against the side of the neck. This pushing action is known as putting and gives the event its name. The shot is put from a throwing circle. The competitor starts at the rear of the circle, facing the opposite way from the direction the shot is to be thrown. In one smooth action, the shot putter glides backwards across the circle with the back leg bent. When the athlete hits the wooden **stop board** at the throwing side of the circle, it is time to turn around, straighten the leg, and propel the shot on its way. If the competitor steps outside the circle while throwing or in the **follow through** then the throw is disqualified. A competition shot can weigh from 2.72 kg to 7.26 kg.

Judy Oakes, Commonwealth champion, releases the shot in perfect style.

The discus

The discus is saucer-shaped and made of wood with a metal edging. The start position is similar to the shot put with the competitor standing at the back of the throwing circle.

ATHLETICS FACTS

The throwing circle diameter

Shot put	**2.135m**
Discus	**2.50m**
Hammer	**2.135m**

Pointers

Young athletes can practise their throwing techniques using lighter implements or even substitutes such as tennis balls and foam rubber javelins.

Holding the discus in one hand, the thrower takes a few swings of the throwing arm and then crosses the circle holding the arm behind while spinning around to gain **momentum**. When the leading foot hits the front of the circle, the discus is released with a sweeping sidearm motion. A discus can weigh from .75 kg to 2 kg.

The hammer

The hammer is a metal ball attached to a handle by a steel wire. The implement has an overall length of about 120 cm. Similar to the shot put event, hammer throwing starts from inside a caged circle. The hammer is held with both hands on the handle. After taking a few practice swings of the hammer, the competitor rotates across the circle. At the front of the circle, the hammer is released with the arms outstretched. The lightest hammers weigh 4 kg and the heaviest ones weigh 7.26 kg.

Learning the javelin. The young athlete follows through.

The javelin

The javelin is a sharpened spear made of metal. The thrower holds the javelin in one hand at shoulder height while building up speed moving along a marked runway. Over the last few strides the javelin is pulled back with the arm fully extended. As the front foot hits the ground for the last time before the throw, the athlete brakes and the power and speed is transferred through the body to the javelin as it is pulled through and released.

Relay racing

A sprint relay changeover by the USA team. Note how both athletes are looking ahead and the outgoing sprinter's arm is outstretched.

The relay races are the only time in athletics where a team competes together in one event. The different combinations of talents and skills make relay races very exciting for the spectators and very nerve-racking for the competitors. In senior competitive athletics there are two main relay races: the 4 by 100 metres relay and the 4 by 400 metres relay. In the first race four teammates each run about 100 metres and in the second, four teammates each run 400 metres. Each of the four relays is called a **leg**. There are relay competitions for both men's and women's teams.

In a relay race, the team members run in turn passing a **baton** on from one runner to the next. This means that learning the technique of the baton change is very important. Four good sprinters with excellent baton changes can often beat a team made up of faster sprinters who haven't practised their changeovers. There is an old saying in athletics that is still true today, 'It's the speed of the baton that counts.'

ATHLETICS FACTS

The name given to the last leg of a relay race is the 'anchor leg'.

The baton needs to pass from runner to runner at the fastest possible speed. This means that the outgoing runner has to know when to start sprinting so that the incoming runner can catch up and pass the baton while they are both in the 22 metre long changeover zone. Only with constant practice at full speed can the exact same changeover point be achieved time after time.

A great moment in British athletics history as Kriss Akabusi beats Antonio Pettigrew (USA) to win the 4 by 440m relay at the 1991 World Championships in Tokyo.

A mark can be placed on the track so the outgoing runner will know that when the mark is passed by the incoming runner it is time to set off. The outgoing runner does not look back but runs a few strides and then confidently places a steady and straight arm out behind to receive the baton. After the changeover is completed, the runner immediately changes the baton to the other hand. If it is the last leg of the race, then the baton can remain in the hand that received it at the changeover.

In the 4 by 400 metre relay where each leg of the race is a lap of the track, the changeover is complicated by the fact that the racers do not need to stay in their own lanes after the first lap and a quarter. This means that both the incoming and outgoing runners have to take care that the handover is not ruined by crowding in the lane. Instead of looking ahead, the outgoing runner looks back, almost until the moment of the changeover, to make sure that all is well. In a race this long, the speed of the pass becomes less important than its reliability.

As well as the competition relays, there are other relay races specially for younger athletes. These are known as shuttle relays. In a shuttle, the runners line up at the start and finish of a sprint race distance, and changeover with their teammates by tapping on the shoulder.

Getting started

Most young people interested in sports can begin training and competing in athletics while they are still at school. If they are talented, they may have a chance to compete against other schools in their town or region. If they are very good they may have a chance to attend special coaching sessions and progress to competing as a member of a junior national squad. Many Olympic and world champions have started out this way.

An important thing for a young athlete to remember is not to specialize in any one event too early. There are numerous examples of top world athletes who have begun their athletics careers in one event only to discover that their real talent was in another event.

Most countries organize international competitions for the best junior athletes. Anyone under twenty can compete as a junior. The European Junior Championships and the World Junior Championships are held in alternate years and are among the most important meets at their level.

The mass start of the 20 kilometre wall at the World Championship in Stuttgart.

If a junior athlete continues at senior level, there are many opportunities for competitions. Athletics clubs exist in most major towns and cities and cater for road and cross-country racing as well as track and field events. In Britain alone there are over 1800 local athletics clubs.

The World Junior Championships are the major championship for athletes under 20 years of age.

The best-known of the major international competitions are the Olympic Games and the World Championships. The World Championships were first held in 1983 at Helsinki in Finland. This competition is now held every two years. For special groups of countries there are also the European Championships and the Commonwealth Games. Like the Olympic Games, both of these are held every four years.

There are also two important **cup competitions**: the European Cup which takes place every year, and the World Cup which is held every four years.

Although athletics is ninety-nine per cent an **amateur** sport, many world-class performers are really **professional** athletes and can get paid quite high sponsorship and appearance money even though most prize money is very low.

For all young athletes there is a clear path that can lead the dedicated and talented to the top of the sport. But remember, the best competitors in any sport are those who can balance the enjoyment and fulfilment they get from their event with the need for fame and success.

Athletics highlights

Athletics competes with soccer as the most popular and widespread sport in the world. The governing body is the International Amateur Athletic Federation (IAAF) which has 204 countries as members. Individual countries and regions also have their own organizations governing the sport in their area.

Down the years field and track athletics have provided the sporting world with some great performances and personalities. In the period leading up to the Second World War, one of the leading US athletes was the runner and jumper Jesse Owens. In 1936 at the Berlin Olympics, this black American won four gold medals. The German Nazi leader, Adolf Hitler, who believed in the supremacy of the white race, was very angry at Owen's success. This tally of four gold medals won in athletics at one Olympic Games was not repeated until the 1984 Los Angeles Olympics when another black American, Carl Lewis, also gained four golds.

Sebastian Coe winning the 1500 metres at the Los Angeles Olympics in 1984. He is the only man in history to win two Olympic 1500 metre titles (he won in 1980 in Moscow).

One of the greatest sporting achievements of the twentieth century was the first running of a mile in under four minutes. Medical student Roger Bannister running at Oxford in England made this breakthrough in 1954. His record was broken again by Australian John Landy only 42 days later.

ATHLETICS FACTS

In 1977 the 92-year-old Duncan McLean, who was known as the Tartan Flash, set a world's best for his age of 21.7 seconds for 100 metres. The race was run at Crystal Palace on a synthetic tartan track!

Today, the sprinting events seem to attract the most attention from the public. During the late 1970s and early 1980s, it was the middle distance running events that seemed to dominate the sport. The world records and Olympic medals won by such athletes as Seb Coe, Steve Ovett and Steve Cram were front page news. Seb Coe's world record for the 800 metres, which he set in 1981, still stands.

The women's sprint record set by American Florence Griffith-Joyner in 1988 has never yet been beaten. Her time of 10.49 seconds for the 100 metres and 21.34 seconds for the 200 metres would beat the best men's record in some countries.

At the 1952 Olympics a husband and wife each won gold medals. The Czech runner Emil Zatopek won three gold medals in the 5000 metres, the 10,000 metres and the marathon. His wife Dana won her gold in the women's javelin event. Since 1983 women athletes have been able to compete in championship marathons. The fastest woman marathoner, Ingrid Kristiansen of Norway, with a time of 2:21:06 has run faster than Zatopek did in winning the gold at the 1952 Olympics!

In 1993 at the World Championships in Stuttgart, Germany, the exploits of the Chinese women distance runners amazed the world. They won the 1500 metres, the 3000 metres and the 10,000 metres races. Later the same year in Beijing, the Chinese athlete Junxia Wang became the first woman to run the 10,000 metres in under thirty minutes.

Junxia Wang (China) is the world champion and record holder at 10,000 metres. She is the only woman to run the distance in under 30 minutes.

Famous faces

As athletes become more fit and the equipment, from the shoes to the track surface itself, changes, world records never seem to stand for more than two or three months, let alone two or three years. One exception to this was the almost unbelievable record held by the famous long-jumper Bob Beamon. At the 1968 Olympic Games in Mexico City, this tall American shocked the world and himself when he jumped the incredible distance of 8.90 metres. This beat the previous world record by an enormous 55cm. Beamon's name appeared in the record books for over twenty years before Mike Powell beat it in Tokyo in 1991. Lynn Davies' British record of 8.23 metres, also made in 1968, still stands.

Sally Gunnell, the only British woman winner of the Grand slam of titles – Olympic, World, European and Commonwealth. She is also the world record holder for 400 metres hurdles and the British team captain.

Linford Christie, one of the greatest sprinters of all time, has won all the major titles available to British athletes: Olympic, World, European and Commonwealth. Since the first World Championships began in 1983, only hurdler Sally Gunnell and decathlete Daley Thompson have also achieved this feat. Born in Jamaica in 1960, Christie came to Britain when he was eight years old. He won his first major title in 1986 – the European Indoor 200 metres sprint. In 1989 he was appointed British men's team captain. Currently the only European athlete ever to run 100 metres in under ten seconds, Christie was honoured by his home borough where the West London Stadium was renamed the Linford Christie Stadium.

Like Christie, Sally Gunnell has also won all four of the available major Grand Slam titles in the 400 metres hurdles. In addition she ran a world record for the 400 metres hurdles at the World Championships in Stuttgart in 1993. Her first major title was as English junior champion long jumper in 1980. Before moving to the 400 metres hurdles, she had success as a sprint hurdler, taking a Commonwealth Games title. Born in Chigwell in Essex in 1966, Gunnell has served as the British women's team captain.

The Ukrainian Sergey Bubka has won many championships and many world records. When he first entered athletics, Bubka competed under the flag of the Soviet Union. Now he competes for the country of his birth, the Ukraine. Bubka has won every World Championship pole vault title since the competition began. He is the only athlete in any event to accomplish this. He is also one of only two men ever to have vaulted over six metres. Bubka was also the Olympic champion at Seoul in Korea.

American Carl Lewis is probably the greatest sprinter of all time. He has also used his great speed and concentration to win four Olympic long jump titles. He first made an impact on the international scene at the World Championships of 1983 where he won three gold medals (100 metres, long jump and relay). A year later, in front of his home crowd in Los Angeles, he won all three again adding another gold in the 200 metres. In 1991 Lewis won what many consider to have been the greatest 100 metres race ever at the World Championships in Tokyo, setting a world record. Born in Birmingham, Alabama USA in 1961, Carl Lewis has jumped over 8.53m 67 times and has run the 100 metres in under ten seconds fifteen times.

The greatest pole vaulter of all time, Sergey Bubka (Ukraine). He holds the world indoor and outdoor records and has won all the World Championships.

Glossary

amateur An amateur sportsperson who takes no money for competing.

approach run This describes the run up taken by an athlete before a jump or throw.

attempt This means a try at doing something.

baton The cylindrical-shaped object that relay racers pass between each other.

cinder This is the material that running tracks used to be made of. It is a coal by-product.

crouch start This is the position that the runners take before the start of a sprint.

cup competition Team competition for clubs and countries for a trophy.

designated The place where something or someone must go.

disqualified In any sport, if you break the rules, you may be barred from competing. This is being disqualified.

echelon A staggered start to ensure every runner covers the same distance on a track that has curves.

facilities This means the equipment and accommodation.

field The area of an athletics ground encircled by the track where all the field events are held.

follow through The continuing movement of the athlete's body after an implement has been thrown.

fouling What happens in jumps and throws when the athlete goes in front of the circle, stop line or take-off board.

implements The things which are thrown in athletics, such as the shot, hammer, javelin and discus.

invalid Not allowed, disqualified.

leading In athletics this word is used to describe the arm or leg that is in front or swinging forward as an athlete moves.

leg In relay racing this means the part of the race run by one of the four team members.

meeting In athletics the words meeting or meet are sometimes used to describe a competition.

momentum Force or speed caused by movement.

Olympic Games The international sporting competition held at a different location every four years. Winter and summer games are held. Athletics are part of the summer Olympics.

pace judgement Being able to judge what the speed is in a race.

pentathlon A five-event competition now replaced by the eight-event heptathlon for women.

professional A professional is a sportsperson who takes money to compete.

relays Races which involve teams of four competing over given distances.

sprints Races where speed is the most important factor.

stadium A stadium is an arena with spectator seating especially constructed for sporting events.

stamina This is the power to continue even when you are tired.

starting block A wedge-shaped object used to hold the foot or feet at a heel-up angle while a racer is in the start position.

stop board A board used in shot put to help stop forward momentum.

straight This is the straight part of an oval-shaped track, so each oval track has two straights.

supple This means flexible and easy to bend.

synthetic A manufactured, not natural, material.

tactics How to perform an event, such as distance races, high jump or pole vault.

take-off board A wooden board used for long and triple jump. If the athlete goes beyond the board a foul is committed.

technique The method and skill used in performing an event.

tension This word describes mental and emotional strain.

track This is the oval-shaped running surface that encircles the field.

trailing In athletics this is used in hurdling to describe the leg that is behind or swinging back as an athlete moves.

Index